Compreh

INFERENCE

LEVEL
D

STECK-VAUGHN
COMPANY
A Subsidiary of National Education Corporation

Executive Editor:	Diane Sharpe
Project Editor:	Melinda Veatch
Design Coordinator:	Sharon Golden
Project Design:	Howard Adkins Communications
Cover Illustration:	Rhonda Childress
Photographs:	©Focus on Sports

ISBN 0-8114-7847-5

6 7 8 9 10 VP 01 00 99 98 97

Making an inference means making a guess. You can make this guess by putting together what you know and what you read. In this book you will make inferences about stories.

You make inferences all the time. Look at the picture. Have you ever received an award? Did you feel happy or proud of yourself? How do you think the people in this picture feel? What helped you make this inference?

What Is an Inference?

An inference is a guess you make after thinking about what you already know. Suppose you are going to see a movie. From what you know about movies, you might infer that you will wait in line to buy a ticket. You will watch the movie on a large screen in a dark theater.

An author does not write every detail in a story. If every detail were told, stories would be long and boring. And the main point would be lost. Suppose you read, "Jane rode her bike to the park." The writer does not have to tell you what a park is. You already know that it is a place where people go to have fun outdoors. From what you know, you might guess that people who go to a park can play ball, swim, or play on the swings. By filling in these missing details, you could infer that Jane went to the park to meet friends for a ball game. You can infer the missing details from what you know.

Try It!

Read this story about Harriet Beecher Stowe. Think about the facts.

◆

Harriet Beecher Stowe lived in the 1800s. At that time some people owned slaves. Stowe knew that slavery was wrong and wanted to speak out against it. She wrote a book called *Uncle Tom's Cabin*. It was published in 1852. It was the story of Tom, a good man who was a slave. It told about how badly slaves were treated. This book made many people think about slavery.

What inference can you make about Harriet Beecher Stowe? Write an inference on the line below.

You might have written something such as "Stowe hoped to help slaves by writing a book about how bad slavery was." You can make this inference by putting together the facts in the story and what you already know. You know that people who have strong feelings about something want to help.

Using What You Know

Read the stories on this page. Look at the sentences in the story and figure out what the story is about. Finally, make an inference about how the person who is telling the story must feel.

People had been giving me funny looks all day long. Finally when I got home, I decided to change into some comfortable clothes. As I took my shirt off, I realized the shirt pocket was on the inside.

I felt _____.

I stopped at the stop sign. I looked both ways and then pressed the pedal to go. When I reached the middle of the street, I saw the other car speeding towards me. The driver didn't even see the stop sign.

I was _____.

It was raining. My friend was still mad at me. I bet she'd never call me again. I watched a movie on TV, but the actor kept reminding me of my friend.

I started to _____.

We cooked hamburgers and hot dogs. All of my friends played ball together. The cake was the biggest one I have ever had. I got five presents.

I felt _____.

Practice Making Inferences

Read each story. Then read the statements after each story. Some are facts. They can be found in the story. Other statements are inferences. Decide whether each statement is a fact or an inference. The first one has been done for you.

◆

Tim and John played basketball together each day after school. One day Tim started shouting that John was not playing fair. John took his basketball and went home. The next day John didn't show up at the basketball court.

Fact	Inference		
○	●	**1.**	**A.** Tim and John were friends.
●	○		**B.** Tim and John played basketball together.
●	○		**C.** John took his basketball and went home.
○	●		**D.** John was angry with Tim the next day.

You can find statements **B** and **C** in the story. So they are facts. You can infer that the boys were friends. But that isn't stated in the story. So statement **A** is an inference. We don't know for sure why John didn't come to the basketball court. So statement **D** is also an inference.

◆

Alfred Nobel was a Swedish inventor. He invented dynamite in 1867. Nobel was worried about how dynamite would be used. He hoped it would be used for peaceful purposes. He established a fund that gave awards each year. These awards are called Nobel Prizes. They are given for works of writing and of science. They are also given to those who have done special things for peace.

Fact	Inference		
○	○	**2.**	**A.** Nobel was an inventor.
○	○		**B.** Nobel was a strong supporter of world peace.
○	○		**C.** Nobel believed that war was bad.
○	○		**D.** Some Nobel prizes are given for writing.

To check your answers, turn to page 62.

How to Use This Book

Read the stories in this book. Answer the questions after each story. You can check your own answers. If you wish, tear out pages 59 through 62. Find the unit you want to check. Fold the answer page on the dotted line to show the correct unit. Line up the answer page with the answers you wrote. Write the number of correct answers in the score box at the top of the page.

You can have fun with inferences. Turn to pages 56 through 58, and work through "Think and Apply."

Remember

In this book you are asked to find facts and to make inferences. Read the story. Then read the statements after the story. Which of these statements can you find in the story? These are facts. Which statements can you infer by thinking about what you've read and what you know? These are inferences.

Hints for Better Reading

◆ As you read keep in mind the difference between facts and inferences.

◆ Think about the facts in the story. Think about what you already know. Make an inference by putting together what you know and what you've read.

Challenge Yourself

Read each story. Mark your answers. Then write one more inference you can make about each story.

1. Trees need special care. They must be planted in a certain way. The roots need a lot of room in order to grow. The hole for the roots must be very wide and deep. The roots grow deep into the earth. And they spread as wide under the ground as the branches do above the ground.

2. It was spring and time to get the garden ready for planting. Chris had a load of dirt delivered to his back yard. For two whole days, Chris shoveled dirt into a wheelbarrow. He put the dirt in the garden. He went back and forth between the dirt pile and the garden. It took many hours and much hard work. On the third day, he saw his neighbor coming over with a wheelbarrow.

3. One rainy day Nan noticed water dripping from the ceiling. That was when she knew she needed a new roof. She asked a few people for their advice. One person told her that putting new shingles over the old roof would make it too heavy. Another person told her that it would be all right to add another layer of shingles.

4. The *Merrimac* was a ship built during the Civil War. The Southern army pulled up an old wooden ship that had been sunk in battle. They put sheets of iron all around its wooden hull. They wanted to use the ship in battles against the North. They thought the iron would protect the ship against cannonballs and gun shells when it was in battle.

5. Nel lives on a farm. She raises chickens for a living. Each morning she goes to the henhouse to collect eggs from the nests. Every week a truck comes to pick up the white eggs for a large grocery store chain in the city. Once every two weeks another truck comes to pick up the brown eggs.

Fact	Inference		
○	○	**1.** **A.**	Tree roots grow underground.
○	○	**B.**	A large tree needs a big hole.
○	○	**C.**	A tree's roots spread as wide as its branches.
○	○	**D.**	Trees must be planted in a special way.

Fact	Inference		
○	○	**2.** **A.**	Chris needed another wheelbarrow.
○	○	**B.**	Chris hoped his neighbor would help.
○	○	**C.**	Chris put the dirt in the garden.
○	○	**D.**	Chris had the dirt delivered.

Fact	Inference		
○	○	**3.** **A.**	Nan needs a new roof.
○	○	**B.**	Two people gave Nan different advice.
○	○	**C.**	A heavy roof might fall into the house.
○	○	**D.**	Nan can't do the job by herself.

Fact	Inference		
○	○	**4.** **A.**	The *Merrimac* was covered with iron.
○	○	**B.**	Wooden ships sank easily in battle.
○	○	**C.**	The *Merrimac* was built during the Civil War.
○	○	**D.**	The *Merrimac* was built in the South.

Fact	Inference		
○	○	**5.** **A.**	People buy more white eggs than brown.
○	○	**B.**	Nel lives on a farm.
○	○	**C.**	Trucks pick up the eggs.
○	○	**D.**	Nel likes raising chickens.

1. In the spring, many farmers put beehives in their fields of fruit trees. Bees collect pollen from the flowers on the trees. They eat the pollen. And as they fly, they spread pollen from flower to flower. In this way, they help the trees produce fruit.

2. The Amazon River provides water to the largest rain forests on Earth. This water helps the trees and plants in these forests grow. The plants help us by making oxygen for the Earth. Over the last thirty years, great parts of these rain forests have been cut down.

3. Many teachers have filmstrips that students can look at on their own. Students read or listen to facts at their own pace when they look at a filmstrip. Filmstrips explain how things work. Often they include charts and figures. The student moves to the next frame when he or she knows all the facts on the frame shown.

4. Atlases are made up of maps. One kind of atlas is a historical atlas. It has maps that show how groups of people or countries have gained or lost land over the years. Some maps tell about trips that explorers have made to different countries. The maps can show mountains, deserts, rivers, and oceans. The maps also give facts about the products each country makes and trades with other countries. Historical atlases cover events from the past to the present.

5. Bill and Sid collect cans. They sell the cans to a recycling center. Lately business has been so good that they have divided their work in half. Bill's area includes a park where teams play baseball every day. Sid collects cans from office buildings and stores.

Fact	Inference		
○	○	**1.** **A.**	Farmers put beehives in their fields.
○	○	**B.**	Bees collect pollen from the flowers.
○	○	**C.**	Farmers need bees in order to grow fruit.
○	○	**D.**	Bees do not eat all of the pollen.

Fact	Inference		
○	○	**2.** **A.**	The Amazon River provides water to the rain forests.
○	○	**B.**	The rain forest plants make oxygen.
○	○	**C.**	Thirty years ago the jungle gave off more oxygen.
○	○	**D.**	The Amazon is a river.

Fact	Inference		
○	○	**3.** **A.**	Filmstrips let students work at their own pace.
○	○	**B.**	Filmstrips often have charts and figures.
○	○	**C.**	Many schools use filmstrips.
○	○	**D.**	Many filmstrips show facts.

Fact	Inference		
○	○	**4.** **A.**	Maps can help people study history.
○	○	**B.**	Some atlases tell about trade.
○	○	**C.**	Atlases are made up of maps.
○	○	**D.**	Some maps tell about past wars.

Fact	Inference		
○	○	**5.** **A.**	Many people drink canned drinks.
○	○	**B.**	Sid's route includes office buildings.
○	○	**C.**	Bill and Sid earn more money now than when they started.
○	○	**D.**	Bill's route includes a park.

1. Pam and Pat tried out for the soccer team. The coach needed only one more player. She needed a good goalie to block the other team's shots. Last year the team lost every game by more than five goals. During tryouts Pam passed the ball well but couldn't block goal shots. As a practice goalie, Pat saved many shots.

2. George Washington wanted the English ships out of Boston Harbor. But he didn't want to attack the ships. He knew that in a battle many people would die. So he asked that large cannons be sent to Boston. When the cannons arrived, the English quickly left the harbor.

3. Bill had a beautiful lawn. It looked like a thick, green carpet. But his next-door neighbor Fred's lawn looked awful. It had weeds and patches of brown grass, and there were some places where grass didn't grow at all. Both Bill and Fred watered their lawns. They also cut the grass once a week. Bill always put fertilizer on his lawn in the fall and spring, but Fred did not.

4. Frank loved to play tennis, and he was on the tennis court every day. Frank could hit the ball very hard. He was a good player. One day he met his friend Jim for a game of tennis. Jim had just started playing tennis. After the game Frank said, "I will help you with your shots, Jim."

5. A radiator keeps the engine of a car cool. Hot water from the engine runs through hoses to the radiator. The radiator has thousands of air openings. Air rushing past the hoses cools the hot water. A fan forces more air into the radiator when the car is stopped or moving slowly.

Fact	Inference		
○	○	**1.** **A.**	The coach picked Pat to be on the team.
○	○	**B.**	A good goalie can help a team win.
○	○	**C.**	Pat and Pam tried out for the soccer team.
○	○	**D.**	Pam could pass the ball well.

Fact	Inference		
○	○	**2.** **A.**	The English were afraid of the cannons.
○	○	**B.**	Washington cared about the people in Boston.
○	○	**C.**	Washington didn't want to attack the ships.
○	○	**D.**	English ships were in Boston Harbor.

Fact	Inference		
○	○	**3.** **A.**	Bill and Fred watered their lawns.
○	○	**B.**	Bill and Fred cut their lawns once a week.
○	○	**C.**	Bill took good care of his lawn.
○	○	**D.**	Grass needs fertilizer to stay green.

Fact	Inference		
○	○	**4.** **A.**	Frank loved to play tennis.
○	○	**B.**	Frank and Jim met for a game of tennis.
○	○	**C.**	Frank won the game.
○	○	**D.**	Jim was not a good tennis player.

Fact	Inference		
○	○	**5.** **A.**	The engine would overheat without a radiator.
○	○	**B.**	Radiators have openings for air.
○	○	**C.**	The air cools the hot water.
○	○	**D.**	Cars produce much heat.

1. Clipper ships were very fast wooden ships. Each ship had a v-shaped hull and many large sails. The front of each ship cut through the ocean like a knife. A clipper ship could cross the Atlantic Ocean in twelve days. Later these ships were replaced by ships with steam engines.

2. Robins have their own territory. Each spring the male robin picks out a large area where there is enough food to feed two birds. This is where he will make a nest. He sings to let other birds know that the space belongs to him. His singing also attracts a female robin that will be his mate.

3. Power windows in a car go up and down with the touch of a button. The car battery sends electricity to a motor that moves the windows. If the car engine isn't on, the windows can't be opened or closed. This could cause problems if you need to roll the windows down, and the person with the car keys is in the store.

4. Before the American Revolution, the English navy owned large parts of American forests. Strong, tall trees grew in these forests. They were used to build English ships. The English did not allow the Americans to cut down these trees.

5. Chicago is one of the few places where people play softball with a 16-inch ball. Most softballs are smaller. The rules for softball are like the rules for baseball. But the players don't use gloves or mitts. The pitcher throws the ball underhand. It is hard to hit a softball a long distance.

Fact	Inference			
○	○	**1.**	**A.**	Clipper ships were very fast.
○	○		**B.**	Steam ships were faster than clipper ships.
○	○		**C.**	Clipper ships had v-shaped hulls.
○	○		**D.**	Wind moved the clipper ships.

Fact	Inference			
○	○	**2.**	**A.**	Robins know how much food they need.
○	○		**B.**	Robins talk to other birds by singing.
○	○		**C.**	Male robins attract mates by singing.
○	○		**D.**	Robins build nests in their territories.

Fact	Inference			
○	○	**3.**	**A.**	A motor moves power windows.
○	○		**B.**	Power windows need electricity to work.
○	○		**C.**	Power windows can cause problems.
○	○		**D.**	You can't roll up power windows by hand.

Fact	Inference			
○	○	**4.**	**A.**	The English navy was very powerful.
○	○		**B.**	America was a part of England.
○	○		**C.**	The English owned large parts of American forests.
○	○		**D.**	Americans could not cut down certain trees.

Fact	Inference			
○	○	**5.**	**A.**	People in Chicago like the 16-inch ball.
○	○		**B.**	Softball is not played with a mitt.
○	○		**C.**	Baseball players need mitts.
○	○		**D.**	Most softballs are smaller than 16 inches.

1. Jason sat in the back of the class. He didn't like to talk or read. One day the teacher told the class that they would act in a play. The teacher read some parts of the play. Jason liked the role of Louis, the baseball player. He wanted to be Louis.

2. Many young people are interested in the past. They can learn facts about the past from their families. Grandparents can give many facts. Ross likes to record his grandfather's stories about growing up on a farm in the early 1900s. Ross shares the stories with his friends. They are always surprised at how people lived during that time. "How could they live without air conditioning?" one friend asked.

3. When you recycle something, you use it again. Paper and glass can be recycled. Some cities have started helping people recycle. People put used paper, plastic, glass, and cans into bins. The city makes sure that these objects aren't just thrown away but are made into new items. Years ago these things were buried. But they took up too much space.

4. The area around the North Pole is covered with ice. In the winter the North Pole points away from the sun. The area of ice around the pole grows larger. In the spring the North Pole gets more sunlight. It becomes warmer. As the air warms up, large blocks of ice break away. They fall into the ocean. We call them icebergs.

5. Many years ago the middle parts of the United States did not get rain. In the spring the farmers planted crops. They expected the rain to make the plants grow. The rain never came. Water wells dried up. It stayed dry for years. The fields turned into hills of dust. Farmers left the land. For many years this land was called the Dust Bowl.

Fact	Inference	
○	○	**1.** **A.** Jason was shy.
○	○	**B.** The teacher read part of the play.
○	○	**C.** Jason liked the role of Louis.
○	○	**D.** Jason likes baseball.

Fact	Inference	
○	○	**2.** **A.** Families pass on their past experiences.
○	○	**B.** Grandparents know about the past.
○	○	**C.** Children are interested in the past.
○	○	**D.** Many things have changed over the years.

Fact	Inference	
○	○	**3.** **A.** Burying trash takes up too much space.
○	○	**B.** People now sort their trash.
○	○	**C.** Many cities now help people recycle.
○	○	**D.** Recycling saves space.

Fact	Inference	
○	○	**4.** **A.** The North Pole changes during the year.
○	○	**B.** The North Pole is darker in the winter.
○	○	**C.** The North Pole is covered with ice.
○	○	**D.** Icebergs come from the North Pole.

Fact	Inference	
○	○	**5.** **A.** Plants need water in order to live.
○	○	**B.** Farmers could not make a living.
○	○	**C.** The fields turned into hills of dust.
○	○	**D.** Rains never came.

1. Each year during the last week in April, the old man began his garden. He planted tomatoes during the second week in May. He weeded the garden as the plants grew. By the middle of summer, the tomatoes were ready to sell. Many people bought them. They liked his red, ripe tomatoes. By Labor Day it was time for the old man to pull up all his tomato plants.

2. Heavy trucks can destroy roads. To protect the roads, states make truck drivers weigh their cargo. They do this on giant scales at weigh stations along the road. The truck drives onto the scale, and its weight is taken. If the truck is too heavy, it is not allowed to drive any farther.

3. A large number of preschools have been set up in the last thirty years. This is because more mothers work during the day. Neither parent can stay at home with the children. They need child care. Many people also believe that preschools are good for young children. In a preschool the children can play and learn from each other.

4. When people work for themselves or someone else, they have to pay a federal income tax. People who make a lot of money must pay more money in taxes than those who don't make much money. People who earn much money can afford to pay more taxes. People who makes less money cannot.

5. Many years ago towns planted elm trees. The elms were beautiful trees. When they were planted on both sides of a street, they formed a leafy, green arch The trees kept both streets and homes cool. Then towns throughout the United States had to cut down their elm trees. The trees became infected with Dutch elm disease.

SCORE

Fact	Inference		
○	○	**1.** **A.**	The old man worked hard to grow tomatoes.
○	○	**B.**	The tomatoes were not good after Labor Day.
○	○	**C.**	He weeded the garden as the plants grew.
○	○	**D.**	He sold tomatoes for a very short time.

Fact	Inference		
○	○	**2.** **A.**	Heavy trucks can hurt roads.
○	○	**B.**	States make drivers weigh their cargo.
○	○	**C.**	Trucks must not be overloaded.
○	○	**D.**	Weigh stations have scales.

Fact	Inference		
○	○	**3.** **A.**	Children can learn from each other.
○	○	**B.**	More mothers work outside the home.
○	○	**C.**	Parents think child care is important.
○	○	**D.**	Many children go to preschools.

Fact	Inference		
○	○	**4.** **A.**	People making more money pay more taxes.
○	○	**B.**	People making less money pay fewer taxes.
○	○	**C.**	Federal income tax is fair.
○	○	**D.**	People who work pay taxes.

Fact	Inference		
○	○	**5.** **A.**	People were sad when the elms were cut down.
○	○	**B.**	Large trees keep homes cooler.
○	○	**C.**	Elm trees are large.
○	○	**D.**	Elm trees were destroyed by disease.

1. The bell had just rung. Everyone was hurrying to the next class. Hernando had his drawings with him when Maria came hurrying around the corner and knocked them out of his hands. "Sorry," Maria mumbled. As Hernando bent to pick up the drawings, Maria said, "Wow, these are really great! I didn't know you could do this."

2. An old story tells about a father and his son who wanted to fly. They made some wings with feathers and wax. They tied the wings onto their bodies. The father told the son to stay away from the sun. Then the father and son flew away. But the son flew too near the sun. He lost his wings and fell into the sea.

3. Fossils are made of animal bones or plants that lived millions of years ago. Plants and animals often sank into mud after they died. The mud kept them from being washed away by water. As time went by, the mud hardened and turned the plants and bones into stone. Now people find fossils that have been buried deep in the ground for millions of years.

4. What can you do with trash and garbage? You can throw it away, or you can reuse some of it. A jar can be a vase for flowers or a place to store jewelry, money, or candy. You can put fruit and vegetable scraps in the garden. You can also save newspapers. They can be made into clean paper.

5. The gym was bright with colored lights. Crepe paper hung from the ceiling, and there was a band playing music. The music was so loud that people couldn't talk to one another. It was crowded in the gym, but no one was playing basketball or wearing gym clothes. All the girls were wearing dresses and flowers. All the boys were wearing suits.

Fact	Inference		
○	○	**1.** **A.**	Maria didn't know Hernando well.
○	○	**B.**	Hernando was carrying his drawings.
○	○	**C.**	Maria was impressed.
○	○	**D.**	Hernando was going to art class.

Fact	Inference		
○	○	**2.** **A.**	The son disobeyed his father.
○	○	**B.**	The father was sad his son fell.
○	○	**C.**	The father and son flew away.
○	○	**D.**	The father and son used feathers.

Fact	Inference		
○	○	**3.** **A.**	Some animal bones are fossils.
○	○	**B.**	Fossils take a long time to form.
○	○	**C.**	A fossil tells about the past.
○	○	**D.**	Something must be very old to be a fossil.

Fact	Inference		
○	○	**4.** **A.**	Some things can be used again.
○	○	**B.**	New paper can be made from old.
○	○	**C.**	A jar can be used in several ways.
○	○	**D.**	Not all garbage needs to be thrown away.

Fact	Inference		
○	○	**5.** **A.**	There was a dance in the gym.
○	○	**B.**	The music was very loud.
○	○	**C.**	Basketball was not being played.
○	○	**D.**	Most people were dancing.

1. Most people learn to sail on a small boat. While they are learning, they keep the boat in a protected spot, such as a harbor. First they learn the names of all the parts of the boat. Then they learn how to turn and move the boat with or against the wind. They also learn what to do if the boat turns over. Once people know how to sail a small boat, with practice they can sail a boat of almost any size.

2. Every day Ricky came home from school and went right to his room. He took his homework with him. When it was dinner time, he came out of his room. Ricky's parents thought he was studying. They were proud of how hard their son was working. They were very surprised when Ricky failed three of his classes.

3. Long ago the Romans had a large army. When the army was not at war fighting for Rome, the soldiers built bridges, walls, and aqueducts. Aqueducts were long bridges that carried water. The Romans built these bridges so they could run water from mountain streams down to their towns. Some of the aqueducts were many miles long.

4. Rubber comes from a rubber tree. White juice called latex drips out of holes in the tree. Today latex is used to make many things, such as rubber gloves and paint. People in Mexico were the first to use latex. One thing they did with latex was to make shoes. They dipped their feet in the latex and let it dry.

5. Megan had practiced her part in the play. She knew her lines backwards and forwards. She was very excited about acting in the play. On the day of the play, she woke up with a terrible sore throat. Her throat hurt too much for her to talk.

Fact	Inference		
○	○	**1.** **A.**	People best learn to sail on a small boat.
○	○	**B.**	It is best to learn to sail in a protected spot.
○	○	**C.**	Sailing takes some skill.
○	○	**D.**	Large boats are harder to sail than small boats.

Fact	Inference		
○	○	**2.** **A.**	Ricky was not studying in his room.
○	○	**B.**	Ricky's parents were angry with him.
○	○	**C.**	Ricky went to his room each day.
○	○	**D.**	Ricky failed three of his classes.

Fact	Inference		
○	○	**3.** **A.**	Roman soldiers built bridges and walls.
○	○	**B.**	Aqueducts were very useful.
○	○	**C.**	Water in aquaducts ran from mountain streams down to towns.
○	○	**D.**	Romans were good at solving problems.

Fact	Inference		
○	○	**4.** **A.**	Some Mexican people made rubber shoes.
○	○	**B.**	People no longer dip their feet in latex.
○	○	**C.**	Rubber comes from a tree.
○	○	**D.**	The people in Mexico had good ideas.

Fact	Inference		
○	○	**5.** **A.**	Megan was excited about the play.
○	○	**B.**	Megan had a sore throat.
○	○	**C.**	Megan had practiced her part.
○	○	**D.**	Megan was not able to act in the play.

1. A baby is helpless when it is born. It cannot walk or feed itself. A baby does not know anything about keeping away from danger. Another person must care for all of a baby's needs. But as the baby grows into a child, it doesn't need other people as much.

2. Rita picked up the crying girl and dusted her off. She quickly took the girl out of the street. Then she went into the street to get the bicycle. She sat down with the girl on the sidewalk in front of the girl's house. She looked at the girl's scraped knee and elbow. Just then the girl's mother came out of the house. Rita checked to make sure the girl was all right before she went on to the library.

3. Matt checked his watch. It was 12:15. He did not have to be back in class until 1:00, so he still had 45 minutes to play. He joined some other people who were playing baseball. After a while, he checked his watch again. The watch still read 12:15.

4. Christy sat on the curb. It was early, and there weren't many cars on the street. The neighborhood was very quiet. In fact, she could hear the train rumble as it ran over the tracks. Usually the noise of the cars was so loud that she couldn't hear the train. Then Christy saw some people leaving for work.

5. Locks help ships move through canals. Two sets of gates make up one level of a lock. Each lock is on a different level. Locks are like stairsteps because one lock is always higher than another. When a ship moves upstream, it goes into the lock. The gate at the front of the ship closes. When the ship is in the lock, the gate behind the ship closes. Then water is pumped into the lock. As soon as the water level in the first lock is equal to that in the next lock, the front gate is opened. The gate behind the ship stays closed. The ship moves up into the next lock.

Fact	Inference	
○	○	**1. A.** Babies need to be taken care of.
○	○	**B.** A baby cannot make its own food.
○	○	**C.** A baby needs less care as it grows into a child.
○	○	**D.** Babies are helpless at first.

Fact	Inference	
○	○	**2. A.** Rita is helpful and caring.
○	○	**B.** The girl had fallen off her bike.
○	○	**C.** Rita got the bike out of the street.
○	○	**D.** The girl's mother took her into the house.

Fact	Inference	
○	○	**3. A.** Matt's watch is not working.
○	○	**B.** Matt knows how to tell time.
○	○	**C.** Matt was playing on the playground.
○	○	**D.** Matt has a watch.

Fact	Inference	
○	○	**4. A.** Christy is up early in the morning.
○	○	**B.** It is louder during the day than in the morning.
○	○	**C.** Christy lives near the train tracks.
○	○	**D.** Christy saw people going to work.

Fact	Inference	
○	○	**5. A.** Locks are used to move ships through canals.
○	○	**B.** Water is pumped into the lock.
○	○	**C.** One gate in a lock always stays closed.
○	○	**D.** Each lock is on a different level.

1. The students painted designs. When they were finished, the teacher told them to look at each painting. She wanted them to find the outline of objects in each design. Some students saw flowers and animals in the pictures. Others saw bottles and boxes. But no one found anything in Bill's picture. He had painted it all black.

2. Schools need sprinklers. A sprinkler is like a shower. Sprinklers are installed in or near the ceilings. If a fire should start, the heat from the fire quickly melts a lead plug on the sprinkler. Once the plug melts, water rushes out of the shower-like heads. The water sprays out over a wide area.

3. Long ago if ships wanted to get from Spain to China, they had to sail around Africa. The trip took many months. Some people felt that there must be a better way. So they built a canal in northern Africa. The canal was like a river across the land. Ships could then sail on the canal across the top of Africa. They didn't have to go all the way around.

4. Airlines didn't have much money to build airports when they first flew planes between countries. So they designed airplanes that could land on the water. The bottom of the planes looked like boats. These planes could land anywhere there was water.

5. The Pony Express carried letters from Missouri to California. Riders rode ten miles and changed horses. They could put saddles on new horses in two minutes. Each rider had to change his horse seven times a day. The Pony Express was replaced by the telegraph. The telegraph sent messages over wires.

SCORE

Fact	Inference	
○	○	**1.** **A.** Bill didn't make a design.
○	○	**B.** The teacher was angry with Bill.
○	○	**C.** Students painted designs.
○	○	**D.** Bill was in an art class.

Fact	Inference	
○	○	**2.** **A.** Sprinklers make schools safer.
○	○	**B.** Schools need sprinklers in case of fire.
○	○	**C.** Sprinklers have heads like showers.
○	○	**D.** Sprinklers can put out fires.

Fact	Inference	
○	○	**3.** **A.** Africa is a large area of land.
○	○	**B.** Water surrounds Africa.
○	○	**C.** Ships can sail on a canal.
○	○	**D.** The canal shortened the trip to China.

Fact	Inference	
○	○	**4.** **A.** It didn't cost much to land on water.
○	○	**B.** Airplanes landed on water.
○	○	**C.** Airlines didn't have much money to build airports.
○	○	**D.** Very few planes land on water today.

Fact	Inference	
○	○	**5.** **A.** The Pony Express was slower than the telegraph.
○	○	**B.** Riders changed horses after ten miles.
○	○	**C.** It was very tiring to be a Pony Express rider.
○	○	**D.** Horses were worn out after ten miles.

1. After the American Revolution, many people still wanted to be under English rule. Some of these people moved to Canada and Nova Scotia. They formed their own government. They called their new land New Brunswick.

2. Power lawn mowers make lawn care easy. Years ago people had to push a mower by hand. The push mower had three long blades that were attached to wheels on both sides. As the wheels turned, the blades spun and cut the grass. It took a long time to cut a lawn, especially when the grass was high. You had to be strong to push a mower like this. Today power lawn mowers come in all sizes. Some are so large that a person can ride on them.

3. Fay left by the back door to go to the garage. She jumped into the car and shut the door. About two minutes later, her mother heard screeching tires and a loud crash. Fay's mother ran to the door. She saw smoke and a hole in the garage door.

4. Robert had helped his grandfather cut hay all day. It had been another long, hot day, and he was glad to drive the tractor into the cool barn. He walked to the porch where his grandfather handed him a large pitcher of lemonade and a glass.

5. Brittany helped her father repaint her room. First they moved all the furniture into the middle of the room. Then they brought in ladders. They spread out old newspapers on the floor. While they were spreading the papers, something caught Brittany's eye. So they started to read the papers.

Fact	Inference		
○	○	**1.** **A.**	Many people still wanted the English to rule.
○	○	**B.**	Some people moved to Canada.
○	○	**C.**	Not everyone was against the English.
○	○	**D.**	New Brunswick was a new land.

Fact	Inference		
○	○	**2.** **A.**	Power lawn mowers cut grass easily.
○	○	**B.**	It is hard to move a push mower.
○	○	**C.**	People ride on some mowers.
○	○	**D.**	Today mowers come in all sizes.

Fact	Inference		
○	○	**3.** **A.**	Fay's mother ran to the door.
○	○	**B.**	Fay backed the car through the garage door.
○	○	**C.**	There was a loud crash.
○	○	**D.**	Fay's mother was worried about Fay.

Fact	Inference		
○	○	**4.** **A.**	Robert was happy to finish the day's work.
○	○	**B.**	Robert had cut hay all day.
○	○	**C.**	They were cutting hay in the summer.
○	○	**D.**	Robert's grandfather liked him.

Fact	Inference		
○	○	**5.** **A.**	They did not begin painting right away.
○	○	**B.**	They didn't want to get paint on the floor.
○	○	**C.**	Old newspapers can be interesting.
○	○	**D.**	They moved the furniture.

1. Pygmies live in small tribes in Africa. Their small size sets them apart from other tribes. Most pygmies grow no taller than five feet. Their lives have stayed much the same over hundreds of years. They live in huts shaped like beehives. For food they gather vegetables and fruit and hunt with nets and spears.

2. Colin had been waiting in line at the store for almost twenty minutes. Just when he was next, a man rushed in and broke in front of Colin. "Excuse me, but I was next," Colin said. The man looked at Colin and said, "That's too bad. I'm in a hurry." Colin noticed that there was a service desk on the other side of the store. He walked over to talk to the woman behind the desk.

3. Biltmore House is the largest house in the world. It has 250 rooms. George Vanderbilt had the house built near Asheville, North Carolina. Vanderbilt was the son of an American family that made a fortune in the railroad business.

4. Karen wanted to buy a new pair of roller skates. She decided to set up a yard sale to earn the money. Karen's mother helped her. They collected things around the house that they no longer wanted. Karen made signs and posted them around her neighborhood. Then they arranged the things on card tables in their front yard. A lot of buyers came to the yard sale.

5. Mammals are animals that feed their young with milk. Pigs are the mammals that have the most babies. A pig can have as many as 34 babies at a time. A mother pig is called a sow. Baby pigs that are less than 10 weeks old are called piglets.

SCORE

Fact	Inference		
◯	◯	**1. A.**	Pygmies are smaller than most people.
◯	◯	**B.**	Pygmies gather fruit and vegetables.
◯	◯	**C.**	Pygmies live in huts.
◯	◯	**D.**	Pygmies hunt with nets.

Fact	Inference		
◯	◯	**2. A.**	Colin planned to complain.
◯	◯	**B.**	A man rushed in front of Colin.
◯	◯	**C.**	Colin did not think the man was fair.
◯	◯	**D.**	The man said he was in a hurry.

Fact	Inference		
◯	◯	**3. A.**	Vanderbilt had the house built.
◯	◯	**B.**	Biltmore House is in North Carolina.
◯	◯	**C.**	Vanderbilt was rich.
◯	◯	**D.**	Biltmore House has 250 rooms.

Fact	Inference		
◯	◯	**4. A.**	Karen liked to skate.
◯	◯	**B.**	Karen was willing to work for money.
◯	◯	**C.**	Karen set up a yard sale.
◯	◯	**D.**	Karen made signs for the yard sale.

Fact	Inference		
◯	◯	**5. A.**	Pigs feed their young with milk.
◯	◯	**B.**	Piglets are very small.
◯	◯	**C.**	Pigs are mammals.
◯	◯	**D.**	A pig can have up to 34 babies at a time.

1. Parkside Hospital was holding a big bike race. Those who entered would help raise money for the hospital. Robin and Gwen decided to enter the five-mile race. As the girls reached the end of the race, Gwen rode her bike over a hole in the road. She fell off and landed on the street. Although Robin was in the lead, she stopped to make sure Gwen was okay.

2. Hummingbirds are the smallest birds. Some hummingbirds weigh less than a dime. They beat their wings very fast. Their wings beat up to 70 times a second. Because they are so active, they feed about once every 10 or 15 minutes. Hummingbirds are the only birds that can fly backwards.

3. A field of daisies grew behind Ellen's house. Ellen knew her neighbor Mrs. Shaw liked daisies. Mrs. Shaw would sometimes tell Ellen stories about when she was a girl long, long ago. Ellen remembered the story Mrs. Shaw told about her straw hat with daisies. It seems the hat blew off Mrs. Shaw's head into a lake. Mr. Shaw hated the hat and refused to get it. Ellen laughed to herself as she remembered the story. She decided to pick a bunch of daisies for Mrs. Shaw.

4. Many books and movies have been written about the story of Robin Hood. Robin Hood was a folk hero who robbed the rich and gave what he took to the poor. Robin Hood is said to have lived in Sherwood Forest. He lived with a band of merry men. Many people have tried to prove he was a real person. But so far no one has been able to show that he really lived.

5. Jake's dad loved to read books about airplanes. One day Jake was at the library. He noticed a new book about airplanes near the check-out desk. "Wait a minute, please," he said to the librarian. He walked over to get the book. "Could you add this to the books I'm checking out?" he asked.

Fact	Inference		
○	○	**1.** **A.**	The race was five miles long.
○	○	**B.**	Robin and Gwen liked to ride bikes.
○	○	**C.**	Gwen fell off her bike.
○	○	**D.**	Robin was a helpful person.

Fact	Inference		
○	○	**2.** **A.**	Hummingbirds are very light.
○	○	**B.**	Hummingbirds can fly backwards.
○	○	**C.**	Hummingbirds beat their wings fast.
○	○	**D.**	Hummingbirds spend a lot of time eating.

Fact	Inference		
○	○	**3.** **A.**	Mrs. Shaw was an older woman.
○	○	**B.**	Mrs. Shaw liked daisies.
○	○	**C.**	Ellen decided to pick daisies for Mrs. Shaw.
○	○	**D.**	Ellen was a caring person.

Fact	Inference		
○	○	**4.** **A.**	Robin Hood is a popular story.
○	○	**B.**	People admire Robin Hood.
○	○	**C.**	Robin Hood cared about the poor.
○	○	**D.**	No one can prove that Robin Hood really lived.

Fact	Inference		
○	○	**5.** **A.**	Jake was checking out books.
○	○	**B.**	Jake was at the library.
○	○	**C.**	Jake's dad liked books about airplanes.
○	○	**D.**	Jake wanted to please his father.

1. George Washington founded the first United States mint. Silver was scarce at the time. So the first president gave his own household silver dishes and candlesticks to the mint. They were melted down and made into the first American coins.

2. Kayla was playing on the jungle gym in the park behind her house. Twice she had called her mom for help. Each time her mom came, Kayla laughed. She said she was just joking. Kayla's mom was very angry with her. Then Kayla fell from the top bar. She called to her mother for help, but her mother did not come.

3. In 1811 David Thompson was exploring the Rockies. He came across a large footprint. It was 14 inches long and 8 inches wide. The footprints were not the prints of any known animal. Some people call the creature Bigfoot. Over 750 people say they have seen the hairy creature. It is said to be 8 feet tall and weigh 400 pounds.

4. The first rays of sun broke through Joy's window blinds. From her apartment she could hear the sounds of the city. A dump truck was collecting garbage. Another truck was making deliveries. Then Joy heard a sound she did not know. She stumbled out of bed to see what it was. Joy looked out her window and smiled. A mother robin was feeding her babies outside the window.

5. Have you ever played with a yo-yo? Yo-yos were first used in the Philippines. They were not used as toys. Instead they were used for protection in the jungle. The word *yo-yo* means "to return" in the Philippine language. Today the yo-yo is a favorite toy in many countries.

Fact	Inference	
○	○	**1. A.** Washington wanted to help the mint.
○	○	**B.** Washington founded the first mint.
○	○	**C.** A mint is where coins are made.
○	○	**D.** At the time, there wasn't much silver.

Fact	Inference	
○	○	**2. A.** Kayla fell from the top bar.
○	○	**B.** Kayla's joke hurt her in the end.
○	○	**C.** Kayla liked to play tricks.
○	○	**D.** Kayla's mom did not like Kayla's game.

Fact	Inference	
○	○	**3. A.** Bigfoot may live in the Rockies.
○	○	**B.** The footprints may have belonged to Bigfoot.
○	○	**C.** Over 750 people say they have seen Bigfoot.
○	○	**D.** Bigfoot may be 8 feet tall.

Fact	Inference	
○	○	**4. A.** Joy heard the sounds of the city.
○	○	**B.** The mother robin was feeding her babies.
○	○	**C.** Joy had never heard baby birds.
○	○	**D.** The baby birds were making loud noises.

Fact	Inference	
○	○	**5. A.** Yo-yos are fun to play with.
○	○	**B.** Yo-yos protected people from wild animals.
○	○	**C.** *Yo-yo* means "to return."
○	○	**D.** Today the yo-yo is a favorite toy.

1. It had been snowing for two hours. Tanya and her mother decided take a walk in the woods. As they walked, everything seemed very still. The ground looked like a field of cotton. Tanya caught a tiny snowflake on the tip of her tongue. She turned and looked at her mother. Fluffy snowflakes dusted her mother's eyelashes.

2. Hot dogs were named by a newspaper cartoonist from Chicago. One day in 1906, cartoonist Tad Dorgan was at a baseball game. A boy came by selling frankfurters. Dorgan drew a picture of the frankfurters. He made them look like small, long dogs on a bun. Under the cartoon he wrote, "Hot dogs."

3. Peter lived next door to Cory. Tiger Rag was Cory's cat. One day Peter's dog chased Tiger Rag up a tree. Tiger Rag clung to one of the top branches for many hours. The next day Tiger Rag was still in the tree. Cory had called Tiger Rag to come down for a long time. But he would not come to her. Finally Peter asked to borrow his father's ladder. He leaned it on the tree and climbed to the top rung. After a few minutes, Tiger Rag grabbed onto Peter's sleeve, and Peter brought the cat down.

4. Everyone knows what a tiger is. And everyone has heard of lions. But do you know what a "liger" is? A liger is a cross between a lion and a tiger. In 1948 the first liger was born in the United States. It was born at the Hagh Zoo in Salt Lake City, Utah. If you had been there at the time, what would you have named it?

5. Marcie loved bananas. She loved banana splits, banana pudding, and banana ice cream. But her favorite way to eat a banana was to simply peel it and eat it. One day she had just enjoyed her favorite food while sitting on the front steps of her house. She left the peel on the steps. An hour later her mother came home. As she climbed the steps to the front door, she noticed the peel. But it was too late.

Fact	Inference		
○	○	**1.** **A.**	It was winter.
○	○	**B.**	Being out in the snow was fun.
○	○	**C.**	Tanya caught a snowflake on her tongue.
○	○	**D.**	Tanya and her mother were walking.

Fact	Inference		
○	○	**2.** **A.**	Hot dogs were first called frankfurters.
○	○	**B.**	Tad Dorgan was a cartoonist.
○	○	**C.**	People liked the new name.
○	○	**D.**	Dorgan's cartoon was printed in the newspaper.

Fact	Inference		
○	○	**3.** **A.**	Peter cared about Cory's cat.
○	○	**B.**	Tiger Rag was up in a tree.
○	○	**C.**	Peter climbed up the ladder.
○	○	**D.**	Peter felt responsible for Tiger Rag.

Fact	Inference		
○	○	**4.** **A.**	A liger is a cross between a lion and a tiger.
○	○	**B.**	Many people don't know about ligers.
○	○	**C.**	Ligers were unusual animals in 1948.
○	○	**D.**	Most ligers live in zoos.

Fact	Inference		
○	○	**5.** **A.**	Marcie left the peel on the steps.
○	○	**B.**	Marcie's mother slipped on the peel.
○	○	**C.**	Marcie loved bananas.
○	○	**D.**	Marcie's mother was angry.

1. In 1947 African Americans did not play with whites on the same team. But Jackie Robinson and the Brooklyn Dodgers changed all that. That first day Robinson was on the baseball field, some people cheered him. But others hissed and booed. By the time he died in 1972, African Americans had become important players in all sports.

2. Brad and his friends were walking home from school. The traffic light had just changed. The "Don't Walk" sign was flashing. His friends kept on walking. But Brad decided to obey the signal. A car screeched to a stop to keep from hitting the boys. A police officer who had been watching walked up to the boys.

3. The Taj Mahal is a beautiful building. It is made of snow-white marble. It stands beside a river in Agra, India. The emperor of India had it built for his wife. She died in 1630 at the age of 39. It took 20,000 men to build the Taj Mahal. They worked for over 22 years. The emperor had planned for a building made of black marble across the river. But it was never built.

4. Acid rain is a growing problem. When factories burn coal, they give off harmful gases. These gases mix with falling rain and make a weak acid. The acid falls into lakes and streams. It kills fish, plants, and many trees. To solve the problem, factories need to put in special equipment that keeps the harmful gases from escaping into the air.

5. Liz stared out the window. She held her head in her hands. Drops of rain splashed on the closed window. As each drop fell, it seemed to run a race to the bottom. Liz thought about the last three days she had spent in bed—sick. Then she imagined herself putting on her yellow raincoat. She pretended she could feel the soft rain on her face. She thought she could even smell the rain.

Fact	Inference		
○	○	**1.** **A.**	At first some people booed Robinson.
○	○	**B.**	Robinson died in 1972.
○	○	**C.**	The Dodgers wanted Robinson to play.
○	○	**D.**	Robinson had great courage.

Fact	Inference		
○	○	**2.** **A.**	Brad's friends did not obey the signal.
○	○	**B.**	The police officer was watching the boys.
○	○	**C.**	Brad obeyed the traffic signal.
○	○	**D.**	The police officer gave the boys a ticket.

Fact	Inference		
○	○	**3.** **A.**	The Taj Mahal is in India.
○	○	**B.**	The Taj Mahal is made of white marble.
○	○	**C.**	The emperor wanted to honor his wife.
○	○	**D.**	The emperor loved his wife very much.

Fact	Inference		
○	○	**4.** **A.**	Acid rain is a costly problem to solve.
○	○	**B.**	Many factories don't have special equipment.
○	○	**C.**	Acid rain kills fish.
○	○	**D.**	Plants cannot live in weak acid.

Fact	Inference		
○	○	**5.** **A.**	Liz was tired of being sick.
○	○	**B.**	Drops of rain splashed on the window.
○	○	**C.**	Liz had a good imagination.
○	○	**D.**	The sky was dark and cloudy.

1. Harry Houdini was known as "the escape king." He could escape from iron boxes, straitjackets, and even bank safes. Some of his most exciting acts used water. People were often afraid that Houdini would not escape. But he always got out safely. He was very strong. And he took good care of his body.

2. Amy's favorite tree had blown over in a wind storm. She had always loved the graceful weeping willow tree. Her dad suggested that she plant another one. They went to a tree farm. They picked out a young tree. When they got home, Amy dug a wide, deep hole. Her dad helped her. Together they placed the new tree gently into the hole. They covered its roots with dirt.

3. Easter Island is in the South Pacific. More than two hundred giant statues stand on the island. They are made of stone. Some are seventy feet tall. Some weigh up to seventy tons. For many years outsiders wondered how the statues were lifted into place. Then Thor Heyerdahl found the answer. He asked some island people to show him their methods. They raised a statue by pushing poles under its head. Then they pushed stones under it until it lifted into place.

4. Mrs. Dai's class had been studying birds. The class decided to go bird watching. They walked along a trail in the woods. Suddenly Mrs. Dai told them to stop a few minutes. When they were quiet, they could hear a loud pecking sound. Mrs. Dai pointed out a woodpecker at the top of a tree.

5. Pocahontas was the daughter of the Native American chief Powatan. She made friends with the English settlers who came to Virginia in the early 1600s. One day their leader John Smith was captured by her tribe. Pocahontas risked her life to save him. She also brought the settlers food to keep them from starving. Later she married John Smith. She helped keep peace between her tribe and the settlers.

Fact	Inference		
○	○	**1.** **A.**	Houdini took good care of his body.
○	○	**B.**	People were amazed by Houdini's escapes.
○	○	**C.**	Houdini could escape from a bank safe.
○	○	**D.**	People like to watch Houdini's acts.

Fact	Inference		
○	○	**2.** **A.**	Amy missed the old willow tree.
○	○	**B.**	Amy's tree was blown over in a storm.
○	○	**C.**	Amy's dad knew she missed the tree.
○	○	**D.**	The new tree was young.

Fact	Inference		
○	○	**3.** **A.**	The statues were hard to raise upright.
○	○	**B.**	Many statues stand on Easter Island.
○	○	**C.**	Easter Island is in the South Pacific.
○	○	**D.**	The people on Easter Island were quite clever.

Fact	Inference		
○	○	**4.** **A.**	The class had to be quiet to hear the woodpecker.
○	○	**B.**	Mrs. Dai wanted her class to hear the woodpecker.
○	○	**C.**	A woodpecker was making the sound.
○	○	**D.**	The class had been studying birds.

Fact	Inference		
○	○	**5.** **A.**	Pocahontas was a brave person.
○	○	**B.**	Pocahontas was a Native American.
○	○	**C.**	Pocahontas cared about the settlers.
○	○	**D.**	The settlers found it hard to find food.

1. The Mayas once lived in southern Mexico and other parts of Central America. They studied the stars and planets closely. They had a strong knowledge of math. Because of this they were able to make a 365-day calendar. Their year had 18 months of 20 days each, plus 5 odd days.

2. "Don't forget to take your raincoat," Lee's mother called out. Lee couldn't wait to get to the birthday party, so she paid no attention. Besides, it wasn't raining now. She put the birthday present in her bike basket and rode off. A few minutes later, she felt a drop on her arm. Within a minute the rain was pouring down.

3. Cows are grass-eating animals. Grass is not easy to chew. Because of this, cows have a special way of making sure they chew it well. They chew a little grass and then swallow it. Then the grass makes its way from the cow's stomach back to its mouth. The cow then chews the grass again. This is called chewing cud.

4. It was a hot summer day. Sue and Ken asked their mom if they could play in the sprinkler. She agreed. As they went outside, she reminded them to turn off the water when they were finished. Ken and Sue ran out to the back yard. They ran in and around the sprinkler for about an hour. Then Sue and Ken got tired of the sprinkler. They decided to ride bikes instead. When they came home, their mother stood at the door. Her arms were crossed in front of her.

5. The Great Wall of China stretches for 1,500 miles. It is 25 to 30 feet tall and about 18 feet across. The wall was started about 215 B.C. It was built over a period of hundreds of years. Some people thought that the wall could be seen from the moon. But in 1969 United States astronaut Alan Bean found that this was not the case. He reported that he could see no buildings while he was on the moon.

Fact	Inference		
○	○	**1.** **A.**	The Mayas made a 365-day calendar.
○	○	**B.**	The Mayas studied the stars and planets.
○	○	**C.**	The Mayas once lived in Central America.
○	○	**D.**	Math was important to the Mayas.

Fact	Inference		
○	○	**2.** **A.**	Lee didn't think it would rain.
○	○	**B.**	Lee's mother told her to take her raincoat.
○	○	**C.**	The birthday present got wet.
○	○	**D.**	Lee paid no attention to her mother.

Fact	Inference		
○	○	**3.** **A.**	Grass is difficult to chew.
○	○	**B.**	A cow's stomach helps it chew the grass well.
○	○	**C.**	Chewing grass over again is called chewing cud.
○	○	**D.**	Grass is an important food for cows.

Fact	Inference		
○	○	**4.** **A.**	Sue and Ken's mom was angry.
○	○	**B.**	Sue and Ken didn't turn off the water.
○	○	**C.**	The back yard was soaked with water.
○	○	**D.**	Sue and Ken decided to ride bikes.

Fact	Inference		
○	○	**5.** **A.**	It took many people to build the Great Wall.
○	○	**B.**	The wall was built over hundreds of years.
○	○	**C.**	Bean could not see the wall from the moon.
○	○	**D.**	The wall is 1,500 miles long.

1. In Greek legends Echo was a pretty maiden. She loved to talk and always wanted to have the last word. But one day Echo's talking got her in trouble. She upset Hera, the queen of the gods, with her endless chatter. So Hera punished Echo. After that Echo could only repeat what others had said. Then she would always have the last word.

2. Most people don't like to do chores around the house. Scientists studied this topic. They found that most people don't like washing dishes. They also do not enjoy cleaning the bathroom.

3. Dolly did not get many new clothes. Usually her clothes were hand-me-downs from big sisters or cousins. On her birthday Dolly got a big surprise. Her mother had taken some of her old clothes and cut them up. Then she had used the bright pieces to sew Dolly a pretty new dress. Dolly was very proud of it. But when she wore it to school, the other kids laughed at her and called her new dress a bunch of rags. Dolly wanted to cry, but she held back her tears.

4. Have you ever had a sunburn? The rays of the sun cause the skin to turn red. The sunburned skill hurts when you touch it. Later the skin usually peels off. Humans suffer sunburn often. But only one other creature, the pig, gets sunburned.

5. P. T. Barnum loved to thrill crowds. He knew what would make them happy. No wonder he is known as the father of the modern circus. He started his "Greatest Show on Earth" in the 1870s. He had the huge elephant Jumbo and other strange creatures. He had clowns and singers, bearded ladies, and other odd acts. People flocked to his circus. Barnum's circus is still in business today.

Fact	Inference	
○	○	**1.** **A.** Echo talked too much.
○	○	**B.** Hera was the queen of the gods.
○	○	**C.** Echo's talking upset Hera.
○	○	**D.** Our word *echo* comes from a Greek word.

Fact	Inference	
○	○	**2.** **A.** Scientists asked people about chores.
○	○	**B.** Most people don't like washing dishes.
○	○	**C.** They would rather use a dishwasher.
○	○	**D.** Most people don't like household chores.

Fact	Inference	
○	○	**3.** **A.** Dolly's family is poor.
○	○	**B.** The new dress made Dolly feel proud.
○	○	**C.** Dolly wore the new dress to school.
○	○	**D.** Her mother wanted to make Dolly happy.

Fact	Inference	
○	○	**4.** **A.** Rays of the sun cause sunburn.
○	○	**B.** Sunburned skin is red.
○	○	**C.** Pigs can get sunburned.
○	○	**D.** Dogs do not get sunburned.

Fact	Inference	
○	○	**5.** **A.** Barnum started his circus in the 1870s.
○	○	**B.** People liked Barnum's circus.
○	○	**C.** Barnum was a smart businessperson.
○	○	**D.** People enjoyed seeing bearded ladies.

1. A huge fire raced through Chicago in 1871. The story goes that a cow in the O'Leary barn kicked over a lantern. Then the hay caught fire, and the flames spread. This story was made up by a news reporter. But the fire was real. It burned for nearly thirty hours. Its flames destroyed more than seventeen thousand buildings.

2. Pickle was a goofy cat, but Sandra loved him. He would often climb trees and then jump on her as she walked below. Sometimes he would hop in the bathtub with her. Of course once he touched the water, he would hop right out again with a howl. Sandra and Pickle spent every afternoon together. Then one day Pickle disappeared. Sandra's parents told her he might have gone to Hollywood to make movies. But Sandra knew better. For weeks she had bad dreams and would cry in her sleep. Pickle never did come back.

3. You probably know that humans have red blood. So do other mammals. But other kinds of creatures have different colors of blood. Insects have yellow blood, and the blood of the lobster is blue.

4. Do you like tomatoes? They taste good on a sandwich or in a salad. But for a long time, people thought tomatoes contained poison. Instead of eating the fruit, people once ate the leaves of the tomato plant. Then they got sick. So they thought the whole plant was bad. For years people would not eat tomatoes because of the fear of poisoning.

5. In college Michael Dell decided to start his own business. He began to sell computers through the mail. His company did very well. So Dell began to design and build his own line of computers. The business kept on growing. Now Michael Dell runs one of the world's largest computer companies.

Fact | Inference

1. **A.** The Chicago fire was in 1871.

○ ○

B. The fire burned for nearly thirty hours.

○ ○

C. Over seventeen thousand buildings were destroyed.

○ ○

D. The reporter didn't know the fire's cause.

○ ○

Fact | Inference

2. **A.** Pickle and Sandra had fun together.

○ ○

B. Cats don't like water.

○ ○

C. Sandra was sad when Pickle disappeared.

○ ○

D. Pickle did not come back.

○ ○

Fact | Inference

3. **A.** Humans have red blood.

○ ○

B. Frogs do not have red blood.

○ ○

C. Lobsters have blue blood.

○ ○

D. Insects have yellow blood.

○ ○

Fact | Inference

4. **A.** People once thought tomatoes had poison.

○ ○

B. Tomato leaves are not good to eat.

○ ○

C. For many years people didn't eat tomatoes.

○ ○

D. Tomatoes do not have poison.

○ ○

Fact | Inference

5. **A.** Dell started his own business.

○ ○

B. Dell first sold computers by mail.

○ ○

C. Dell likes working with computers.

○ ○

D. Dell's company is now very large.

○ ○

1. Dogs are sometimes called "man's best friend," but some dogs are friendlier than others. Some dogs bite many more people than others do. The kind of dog that bites the most is the German police dog. Poodles also often bite people. Sheepdogs, on the other hand, do not bite much at all.

2. Arachne was a skilled weaver. She told everyone she was the best weaver in the world. This claim upset Athena, the Greek goddess of wisdom. Athena had taught humans how to weave. So she thought her weaving was the best. Athena and Arachne then had a weaving contest. When the goddess saw that the human could weave as well as she could, she grew angry. She made Arachne feel great guilt and shame for trying to match the gods. Arachne was so ashamed that she hung herself. But the goddess felt pity for Arachne and changed her into a spider. Then she could weave her lovely designs forever.

3. A new one-dollar coin was made in 1979. It showed the face of Susan B. Anthony. She was a leader in the fight for women's rights. But the new coin caused many problems. It was about the same size as a quarter. So people often confused the two coins. Many merchants refused to accept the coin. So the dollar coin was not used very often.

4. Willy and Louis were starting to get scared. The sun was going down, and the woods around them were growing dark. The two boys were lost! They had been walking for hours, looking for their way out. But they noticed they were only going in circles. Now they nervously watched the shadows grow longer around them.

5. The longest bridge in the world is in England. It crosses the Humber River near Hull. The bridge was built in 1981 and is almost a mile long.

Fact	Inference		
○	○	**1.** **A.**	German police dogs are not good pets.
○	○	**B.**	Poodles often bite people.
○	○	**C.**	Sheepdogs are friendly.
○	○	**D.**	Dogs are called "man's best friend."

Fact	Inference		
○	○	**2.** **A.**	Athena taught humans to weave.
○	○	**B.**	Arachne liked to weave.
○	○	**C.**	Athena changed Arachne into a spider.
○	○	**D.**	Arachne could weave as well as Athena.

Fact	Inference		
○	○	**3.** **A.**	Susan B. Anthony's face was on a coin.
○	○	**B.**	The dollar coin was not made after 1979.
○	○	**C.**	People confused the new coin with a quarter.
○	○	**D.**	Store owners did not like the new coin.

Fact	Inference		
○	○	**4.** **A.**	The boys wanted someone to come find them.
○	○	**B.**	The sun was going down.
○	○	**C.**	Willy and Louis were lost.
○	○	**D.**	The boys had not explored the woods before.

Fact	Inference		
○	○	**5.** **A.**	The world's longest bridge is in England.
○	○	**B.**	The bridge is almost a mile long.
○	○	**C.**	The Humber River is very wide.
○	○	**D.**	The bridge took a long time to build.

1. Do you have to make your bed every day? Of course you don't really make the bed; you just straighten the sheets. The early Romans made beds by putting straw into cloth sacks. The straw then had to be removed every day to dry. So people once really did make their beds every day, and that's where we got the saying.

2. Scientists have done studies on the age of the earth and the moon. They believe the earth was formed more than four billion years ago. Tests on moon rocks show that the moon is a bit older than the earth.

3. Have you ever seen a bullfight? A person stands in a large ring and waves a red cape at a bull. Then the bull runs at the cape, and the person scampers out of the way. You might think that the red color of the cape makes the bull angry, but this is not true. In fact the bull is colorblind, so it cannot tell red from other colors. The bull charges at the motion of the cape, not the color of it.

4. The ad in the comic book promised big money and great prizes. Ginny was excited as she cut out the order form. She dreamed of all the neat things she could get by selling greeting cards. For selling only five hundred boxes, she could win a new bike. But when the cards arrived, Ginny found her job to be very hard. She could only sell four boxes of cards. Her great prize turned out to be a toy whistle.

5. Medusa was a monster in Greek legends. She was once a beautiful woman. But she upset Athena, the goddess of wisdom. In anger the goddess turned her into an ugly creature with wings. Her hair became a nest of squirming snakes. Her face was so horrible that those who looked at it were turned to stone.

Fact	Inference		
○	○	**1.** **A.**	The early Romans made beds of straw.
○	○	**B.**	The straw got damp during the night.
○	○	**C.**	Sleeping on damp beds was not comfortable.
○	○	**D.**	Today people don't sleep on straw beds.

Fact	Inference		
○	○	**2.** **A.**	Scientists have studied the age of the moon.
○	○	**B.**	Tests were done on moon rocks.
○	○	**C.**	People have travelled to the moon.
○	○	**D.**	Tests were done on the earth's rocks.

Fact	Inference		
○	○	**3.** **A.**	In a bullfight a person stands in a ring.
○	○	**B.**	Red capes are used in bullfights.
○	○	**C.**	Bulls are colorblind.
○	○	**D.**	A bull would charge a green cape.

Fact	Inference		
○	○	**4.** **A.**	Ginny thought selling cards would be easy.
○	○	**B.**	The ad in the comic book fooled Ginny.
○	○	**C.**	Ginny wanted a new bike.
○	○	**D.**	The prize Ginny got was a whistle.

Fact	Inference		
○	○	**5.** **A.**	Medusa was a monster.
○	○	**B.**	People were afraid of Medusa.
○	○	**C.**	Athena was the goddess of wisdom.
○	○	**D.**	Medusa had snakes for hair.

1. Cheryl had never tried to fix her bicycle before. But her bike had a flat tire, and it needed to be fixed. No one else had offered to help, so Cheryl decided to try to fix the flat tire herself.

2. You probably have heard of Groundhog Day. It falls on February 2 each year. On that day a groundhog is supposed to come out of its hole in the ground. If it sees its shadow, winter is supposed to go on for six more weeks. If it does not see its shadow, spring is supposed to arrive soon. But a study showed that the groundhog idea works only about one fourth of the time.

3. Baseball is called the national game of the United States. Most people think the game was made up by Abner Doubleday. He lived in Cooperstown, New York. For that reason baseball was called the "New York game" in its early days.

4. Lonnie had never met his cousin Floyd, but he knew he wouldn't like him when he did. He had heard that Floyd liked to poke people and push them down. When his aunt's car drove up, Lonnie did not wait around to meet Floyd. Instead he ran out the back door and into the cornfield. The day was very hot, and the green cornstalks flashed by as Lonnie ran. Soon he stumbled and fell, his head pounding. He was still there when his mother and Floyd found him later. As Floyd helped him back to the house, Lonnie thought that Floyd wasn't such a bad guy after all.

5. Every 10 years the United States counts all the people in the country. This count is called the census. The first census was taken in 1790. It showed that 4 million people lived here then. Now there are about 250 million people in the United States.

Fact	Inference	
○	○	**1. A.** Cheryl wasn't sure she could fix her bike.
○	○	**B.** The bike had a flat tire.
○	○	**C.** Cheryl wanted to ride her bike.
○	○	**D.** No one else offered to help.

Fact	Inference	
○	○	**2. A.** Groundhog Day is February 2.
○	○	**B.** Many people believe that groundhogs know when spring is coming.
○	○	**C.** Spring comes at a different time each year.
○	○	**D.** Groundhogs can't really guess the weather.

Fact	Inference	
○	○	**3. A.** Many Americans like to play baseball.
○	○	**B.** Abner Doubleday lived in New York.
○	○	**C.** Baseball was once called the "New York game."
○	○	**D.** Abner Doubleday liked playing sports.

Fact	Inference	
○	○	**4. A.** Lonnie and Floyd are cousins.
○	○	**B.** Floyd hadn't been to Lonnie's house before.
○	○	**C.** Lonnie was afraid to meet Floyd.
○	○	**D.** Floyd helped Lonnie back to the house.

Fact	Inference	
○	○	**5. A.** The census is taken every ten years.
○	○	**B.** The first census was in 1790.
○	○	**C.** Four million people lived here in 1790.
○	○	**D.** Taking the census was quicker in 1790.

1. Daniel Boone was an American pioneer. He was born in 1734. As a young man, Boone fought in the French and Indian Wars. Then he decided to move west. He led a group of people to Kentucky. On the way he helped to lay out the Wilderness Road. Later he moved west again. This time he journeyed to Missouri. Boone died there in 1820.

2. Have you ever been told to get your elbows off the table? Some people think that elbows on the table during a meal shows bad manners. This idea is many years old. Dining tables used to be crowded. A person's elbows on the table often got in the way. Other people trying to eat sometimes got angry. Even now you could cause an accident with your elbows on the table.

3. The smell of liver made Wally hold his nose. And he thought he would be sick each time he had to taste spinach. Yet there before him sat those two foods, just waiting to be eaten. When his mother left the room, Wally dashed to the window. He scraped his plate clean behind the curtains and hurried back to his seat. When his mother returned, she was surprised at how quickly he had finished his meal. Wally only grinned nervously.

4. In Roman legends Cupid was the god of love. He was a young, winged boy with a bow and arrows. Cupid would shoot his arrows at both the gods and humans. Those struck by his arrows would fall in love instantly.

5. Gwendolyn Brooks is a poet. She was born in Kansas. But she grew up in Chicago. She began to write poems when she was only 13. In 1950 Brooks won the Pulitzer Prize. She won the award for her book of poems called *Annie Allen*. She was the first African American woman to receive this honor.

Fact	Inference	
○	○	**1. A.** Daniel Boone was born in 1734.
○	○	**B.** He liked adventure and excitement.
○	○	**C.** The Wilderness Road goes to Kentucky.
○	○	**D.** Daniel Boone died in Missouri.

Fact	Inference	
○	○	**2. A.** Elbows on the table can be dangerous.
○	○	**B.** Dining tables used to be crowded.
○	○	**C.** In the past, people had larger families.
○	○	**D.** People got angry about elbows on the table.

Fact	Inference	
○	○	**3. A.** Wally doesn't like liver or spinach.
○	○	**B.** Wally's mother was surprised he had finished.
○	○	**C.** Wally scraped his plate behind the curtains.
○	○	**D.** Wally was supposed to eat liver and spinach.

Fact	Inference	
○	○	**4. A.** Cupid was the god of love.
○	○	**B.** Cupid had a bow and arrows.
○	○	**C.** Cupid's arrows made people fall in love.
○	○	**D.** The arrows were very powerful.

Fact	Inference	
○	○	**5. A.** Gwendolyn Brooks likes to write poems.
○	○	**B.** She was born in Kansas.
○	○	**C.** Brooks won the Pulitzer Prize in 1950.
○	○	**D.** Her poems are very good.

1. The English Channel divides England from Europe. One day in 1926, a young woman stood by the channel. She made up her mind to be the first woman to swim across it. Her name was Gertrude Ederle. The swim was hard and rough, but she finished the trip. She swam the 35 miles in less than 15 hours. Her time set a new world record.

2. Galveston is a small island off the coast of Texas. In 1900 a great storm destroyed the place. A hurricane blew in from the Gulf of Mexico. A tidal wave covered the island. Thousands of homes were ruined. More than 800 people died. After the storm people returned to the island. Then a seawall was built to hold back the waters of the gulf.

3. Rick wanted a shiny new skateboard, but he didn't have the money to buy one. He asked his parents for the money, but they told him to get a job. So Rick finally asked a neighbor if he could mow her lawn. She agreed, and soon Rick got other jobs, too. Rick found he really didn't mind working, either.

4. Cleopatra lived more than 2,000 years ago. At the age of 18, she became the queen of Egypt. She ruled with her brothers, but both of them died. Cleopatra then became the only ruler of her land. She was not a great queen. She taxed her people heavily, too. But she held control of the throne until her death at the age of 39.

5. Arbor Day is now held the last Friday in April. On this day people gather to plant new trees. The first Arbor Day was held in the 1870s in Nebraska. At that time people planted trees for their beauty and shade.

Fact	Inference		
○	○	**1.** **A.**	A channel divides England from Europe.
○	○	**B.**	Gertrude Ederle liked to swim.
○	○	**C.**	The long swim made Ederle very tired.
○	○	**D.**	Ederle was a fast swimmer.

Fact	Inference		
○	○	**2.** **A.**	A great storm struck Galveston in 1900.
○	○	**B.**	Not everyone had time to leave the island.
○	○	**C.**	Galveston is on the Texas coast.
○	○	**D.**	A seawall was built after the storm.

Fact	Inference		
○	○	**3.** **A.**	At first Rick didn't want to work.
○	○	**B.**	Rick's parents wanted him to be responsible.
○	○	**C.**	Rick mowed his neighbor's lawn.
○	○	**D.**	Rick enjoyed having his own money.

Fact	Inference		
○	○	**4.** **A.**	Cleopatra first ruled with her brothers.
○	○	**B.**	She was the queen of Egypt.
○	○	**C.**	The people of Egypt did not like Cleopatra.
○	○	**D.**	Cleopatra died at age 39.

Fact	Inference		
○	○	**5.** **A.**	Arbor Day is held in April.
○	○	**B.**	The people in Nebraska liked trees.
○	○	**C.**	Trees give beauty and shade.
○	○	**D.**	The first Arbor Day was in the 1870s.

Think and Apply

Rhonda's Story

The teacher wrote the date for the next science test on the chalkboard. Rhonda copied the date for the test in her assignment notebook. She thought back to the last science test she had taken just a few weeks ago. Rhonda got a sick feeling in her stomach. She didn't do well on that test. But she would not make the same mistake again. This time she was going to study! The test was in one week, so Rhonda had plenty of time. She decided it would be easier if she studied with a partner. The next day at school she asked some of her friends if they could help her study. But they were all too busy. Rhonda worried that she wouldn't be able to find someone to help her. Then a few days before the test, Rhonda ate lunch with a new girl in school named Jill. Rhonda told Jill her problem. Jill offered to help. The two girls got together to study two days before the test. They worked hard for several hours. Then the night before the test, Rhonda studied again by herself. She felt that she was ready for the test.

1. Why did Rhonda want to study for the science test?

   _____

2. How did Rhonda probably do on the test?

   _____

3. What kind of person was Jill?

   _____

4. How did Rhonda probably feel when Jill offered to help?

   _____

The Next Step

Read the first two sentences in each item. Then decide what will happen next. Write your answer for each item on the line below the sentences. The first one has been done for you.

1. The driver didn't see the traffic light turn red.
   The tires screeched as they slid on the street.

   There was an accident.

2. Marty made a peanut butter and jelly sandwich.
   He poured a glass of milk.

3. The ground began to shake, and there was a rumbling noise.
   Clouds of ash blew out of the volcano.

4. The fire alarm rang at the school.
   All of the students quickly lined up in their classrooms.

5. Yuki put the new lightbulb into the socket.
   She flipped the switch to the on position.

6. Valisha found a seat in the movie theater.
   Soon the lights were turned off in the theater.

7. Ned set his clock and turned on the alarm.
   He fell fast asleep.

To check your answers, turn to page 62.

Behind the Story

Read each story. Write your answers in complete sentences on the lines below the questions.

1. Jessica got a letter that said she could go to summer camp. She ran and told her parents right away. Then she called several of her friends and told them. Later that day Jessica wrote her grandparents a letter. She told them about all the things that she would do at camp.

    How does Jessica feel about going to summer camp?

    _____

2. Every Saturday Mark does volunteer work at the retirement home. Sometimes he just sits and talks to the people who live there. Other times he takes them to places such as the library.

    What kind of person is Mark?

    _____

3. Harry wanted to bake a cake for his girlfriend. He started making the cake batter, but suddenly he stopped what he was doing. He jumped into his car and drove to the store. When Harry got back, he opened a new bag of sugar, and he finished mixing the cake batter. He poured it into a pan and stuck it in the oven.

    Why did Harry go to the store?

    _____

4. Beth was excited about reading her new book. She hopped into bed and turned on her reading light. It was getting late, and her eyelids felt heavy, but Beth didn't want to stop reading.

    What did Beth probably do next?

    _____

To check your answers, turn to page 62.

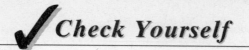

Check Yourself

Unit 1 pp. 6-7	Unit 2 pp. 8-9	Unit 3 pp. 10-11	Unit 4 pp. 12-13	Unit 5 pp. 14-15	Unit 6 pp. 16-17	Unit 7 pp. 18-19	Unit 8 pp. 20-21
1.	**1.**	**1.**	**1.**	**1.**	**1.**	**1.**	**1.**
A. F	A. F	A. I	A. F	A. I	A. I	A. I	A. I
B. I	B. F	B. I	B. I	B. F	B. I	B. F	B. I
C. F	C. I	C. F	C. F	C. F	C. F	C. I	C. I
D. F	D. I	D. F	D. I	D. I	D. I	D. I	D. I
2.	**2.**	**2.**	**2.**	**2.**	**2.**	**2.**	**2.**
A. I	A. F	A. I	A. I	A. I	A. F	A. I	A. I
B. I	B. F	B. I	B. I	B. F	B. F	B. I	B. I
C. F	C. I	C. F	C. F	C. F	C. I	C. F	C. F
D. F	D. F	D. F	D. F	D. I	D. F	D. F	D. F
3.	**3.**	**3.**	**3.**	**3.**	**3.**	**3.**	**3.**
A. F	A. F	A. F	A. F	A. F	A. F	A. F	A. F
B. F	B. F	B. F	B. I	B. F	B. I	B. I	B. I
C. I	C. I	C. I	C. F	C. F	C. I	C. I	C. F
D. I	D. F	D. I	D. I	D. I	D. I	D. I	D. I
4.	**4.**	**4.**	**4.**	**4.**	**4.**	**4.**	**4.**
A. F	A. I	A. F	A. I	A. I	A. F	A. I	A. F
B. I	B. F	B. F	B. I	B. I	B. F	B. F	B. I
C. F	C. F	C. I	C. F	C. F	C. I	C. F	C. F
D. I	D. I	D. I	D. F	D. I	D. F	D. I	D. I
5.	**5.**	**5.**	**5.**	**5.**	**5.**	**5.**	**5.**
A. I	A. I	A. I	A. I	A. I	A. I	A. I	A. F
B. F	B. F	B. F	B. F	B. I	B. I	B. F	B. F
C. F	C. I	C. F	C. I	C. F	C. I	C. F	C. F
D. I	D. F	D. I	D. F	D. F	D. I	D. I	D. I

Unit **9** pp. 22-23	Unit **10** pp. 24-25	Unit **11** pp. 26-27	Unit **12** pp. 28-29	Unit **13** pp. 30-31	Unit **14** pp. 32-33	Unit **15** pp. 34-35	Unit **16** pp. 36-37
1.	**1.**	**1.**	**1.**	**1.**	**1.**	**1.**	**1.**
A. F	A. I	A. F	A. I	A. F	A. I	A. I	A. F
B. I	B. I	B. F	B. F	B. I	B. F	B. I	B. F
C. F	C. F	C. I	C. F	C. F	C. I	C. F	C. I
D. F	D. I	D. I	D. F	D. I	D. F	D. F	D. I
2.	**2.**	**2.**	**2.**	**2.**	**2.**	**2.**	**2.**
A. I	A. I	A. I	A. I	A. I	A. F	A. I	A. F
B. I	B. I	B. I	B. F	B. F	B. I	B. F	B. F
C. F	C. F	C. F	C. I	C. F	C. I	C. I	C. F
D. I	D. I	D. F	D. F	D. I	D. I	D. I	D. I
3.	**3.**	**3.**	**3.**	**3.**	**3.**	**3.**	**3.**
A. I	A. I	A. F	A. F	A. I	A. I	A. I	A. F
B. I	B. I	B. I	B. F	B. F	B. I	B. F	B. F
C. I	C. F	C. F	C. I	C. F	C. F	C. F	C. I
D. F	D. I	D. I	D. F	D. I	D. F	D. I	D. I
4.	**4.**	**4.**	**4.**	**4.**	**4.**	**4.**	**4.**
A. I	A. I	A. I	A. I	A. I	A. F	A. F	A. I
B. I	B. F	B. F	B. I	B. I	B. F	B. I	B. I
C. I	C. F	C. I	C. F	C. I	C. I	C. I	C. F
D. F	D. I	D. I	D. F	D. F	D. I	D. I	D. I
5.	**5.**	**5.**	**5.**	**5.**	**5.**	**5.**	**5.**
A. F	A. I	A. I	A. I	A. F	A. I	A. F	A. I
B. F	B. F	B. I	B. I	B. F	B. I	B. I	B. F
C. I	C. I	C. I	C. F	C. F	C. F	C. F	C. I
D. F	D. I	D. F	D. F	D. I	D. F	D. I	D. I

Unit 17 pp.38-39	Unit 18 pp. 40-41	Unit 19 pp. 42-43	Unit 20 pp. 44-45	Unit 21 pp. 46-47	Unit 22 pp. 48-49	Unit 23 pp. 50-51	Unit 24 pp. 52-53	Unit 25 pp. 54-55
1.	**1.**	**1.**	**1.**	**1.**	**1.**	**1.**	**1.**	**1.**
A. F	A. F	A. I	A. F	A. I	A. F	A. I	A. F	A. F
B. I	B. F	B. F	B. F	B. F	B. I	B. F	B. I	B. I
C. F	C. F	C. F	C. F	C. I	C. I	C. I	C. I	C. I
D. I	D. I	D. I	D. I	D. F	D. I	D. F	D. F	D. I
2.	**2.**	**2.**	**2.**	**2.**	**2.**	**2.**	**2.**	**2.**
A. I	A. I	A. I	A. I	A. F	A. F	A. F	A. I	A. F
B. F	B. F	B. F	B. I	B. I	B. F	B. I	B. F	B. I
C. I	C. I	C. I	C. I	C. F	C. I	C. I	C. I	C. F
D. F	D. F	D. F	D. F	D. F	D. I	D. I	D. F	D. F
3.	**3.**	**3.**	**3.**	**3.**	**3.**	**3.**	**3.**	**3.**
A. I	A. F	A. I	A. F	A. F	A. F	A. I	A. I	A. I
B. F	B. I	B. F	B. I	B. I	B. F	B. F	B. F	B. I
C. F	C. F	C. F	C. F	C. F	C. F	C. F	C. F	C. F
D. I	D. I	D. I	D. F	D. I	D. I	D. I	D. I	D. I
4.	**4.**	**4.**	**4.**	**4.**	**4.**	**4.**	**4.**	**4.**
A. F	A. I	A. F	A. F	A. I	A. I	A. F	A. F	A. F
B. I	B. I	B. F	B. I	B. F	B. I	B. I	B. F	B. F
C. I	C. I	C. F	C. F	C. F	C. I	C. I	C. F	C. I
D. F	D. F	D. I	D. I	D. I	D. F	D. F	D. I	D. F
5.	**5.**	**5.**	**5.**	**5.**	**5.**	**5.**	**5.**	**5.**
A. I	A. I	A. F	A. F	A. F	A. F	A. F	A. I	A. F
B. I	B. F	B. I	B. F	B. F	B. I	B. F	B. F	B. I
C. I	C. F	C. I	C. I	C. I	C. F	C. F	C. F	C. F
D. I	D. F	D. I	D. F	D. I	D. F	D. I	D. I	D. F

Practice Making Inferences, Page 4

2. A. F
   B. I
   C. I
   D. F

Rhonda's Story, Page 56

Possible answers include:

1. Rhonda wanted to make a better grade on the next test.
2. Rhonda probably did well on the test.
3. Jill was helpful and kind.
4. Rhonda was probably happy and relieved when Jill offered to help.

The Next Step, Page 57

2. Marty ate the sandwich and drank the milk.
3. The volcano erupted.
4. The students left the school building.
5. The lightbulb lit up.
6. The movie started.
7. The alarm went off and Ned woke up.

Behind the Story, Page 58

Possible answers include:

1. Jessica is happy and excited about going to camp.
2. Mark is kind, caring, and thoughtful.
3. Harry went to the store to get sugar for the cake.
4. Beth fell asleep with the light on and the book open.